Michigan
History

Marcia Schonberg

Heinemann Library
Chicago, Illinois

© 2004 Heinemann Library
a division of Reed Elsevier Inc.
Chicago, Illinois

Customer Service 888-454-2279

Visit our website at www.heinemannlibrary.com

Designed by Heinemann Library
Photo research by Jill Birschbach and Kathy Creech
Printed in the United States by Lake Book
   Manufacturing, Inc.

08 07 06 05 04
10 9 8 7 6 5 4 3 2 1

Library of Congress
Cataloging-in-Publication Data
Schonberg, Marcia.
  Michigan history / by Marcia Schonberg.
     v. cm. -- (Heinemann state studies)
Includes bibliographical references and index.
Contents: Meeting of two worlds, to 1620 --
Explorers and native
Americans in Michigan, 1585-1763 -- Revolution and the new nation,
1763-1815 -- Building roads to statehood, 1816-1849 -- Civil War and
reconstruction, 1850-1865 -- Michigan's industrial growth, 1866-1918 --
The Great Depression and World War II, 1929-1945 -- Modern Michigan,
1945 to today.
  ISBN 1-4034-0659-6 -- ISBN 1-4034-2677-5 (pbk.)
  1. Michigan--History--Juvenile literature. [1. Michigan--History.] I.
Title. II. Series.
  F566.3.S36 2004
  977.4--dc22   2003012286

Acknowledgments
The author and publishers are grateful to the following for permission to reproduce copyright material:
Title page (L-R) Robert P. Carr/Bruce Coleman Inc., State Archives of Michigan, Phil Schermeister/Corbis; contents page, p. 41t Kit Kittle/Corbis; pp. 5, 18 maps.com/Heinemann Library; pp. 6, 11, 13, 16, 31, 34b, 35t, 38b, 40, 42 Bettmann/Corbis; p. 7 Robert P. Carr/Bruce Coleman Inc.; p. 8 Historical Picture Archive/Corbis; pp. 9, 10, 14, 21, 26, 44 Kimberly Saar/Heinemann Library; p. 17 James L. Amos/Corbis; p. 19 Burton Historical Collection/Detroit Public Library; p. 21 The Detroit News Archives; p. 22 Joseph Sohm/ChromoSohm Inc./Corbis; pp. 23, 30b, 34t State Archives of Michigan; p. 24 Muskegon County Museum; p. 25 Richard Carver; p. 27t Dennis Cox/WorldViews; p. 27b Library of Congress; pp. 28, 30t, 32, 35b, 36b, 38t, 39 Corbis; p. 29 Medford Historical Society Collection/Corbis; p. 33 Phil Schermeister/Corbis; p. 36t Courtesy of the W. K. Kellogg Foundation; p. 41b Hulton Archive/Getty Images; p. 43 Mark E. Gibson/Corbis

Cover photographs by (top, L-R) Medford Historical Society Collection/Corbis, W. Cody/Corbis, Hulton Archive/Getty Images, Bettmann/Corbis; (main) Bettmann/Corbis

The publisher would like to thank expert reader Francis X. Blouin Jr., director of the Bentley Historical Society in Ann Arbor.

Special thanks to Alexandra Fix and Bernice Anne Houseward for their curriculum guidance.

Some words are shown in bold, **like this.** You can find out what they mean by looking in the glossary.

Contents

Meeting of Two Worlds, to 1620

The story of Michigan's history begins about 15,000 years ago. A huge **glacier** slowly pushed back and forth, scraping and forming North America, including the region that would become the state of Michigan. The tremendous size and weight of the glacier left **fertile** soil in some places and ridges and holes in others. Some of these holes became lakes in and around Michigan. The largest ones became the Great Lakes. Grooves that caught the melting glacial water formed Michigan's rivers. The grinding glacier left behind rich soil for flat farmland in the Lower Peninsula and high hills and u-shaped valleys in the Upper Peninsula.

Prehistoric nomads arrived in North America following the last **Ice Age.** These early nomads traveled great distances, coming to North America all the way from Asia. They walked across the Bering Strait. During this time, the Bering Strait was a land bridge called Beringia that connected the two continents of Asia and North America. As the glaciers melted years later, the Bering Strait was covered by water.

EARLY EXPLORERS

Michigan's first people left no written records. However, they did leave unwritten clues about their lives, such as bones and arrow points. The bones came from **mastodon** and **caribou.** Scientists also learned that the earliest settlers found flint, a very hard stone. Marks left on the bones suggest that these early hunters used weapons and tools created from flint.

Migration Routes

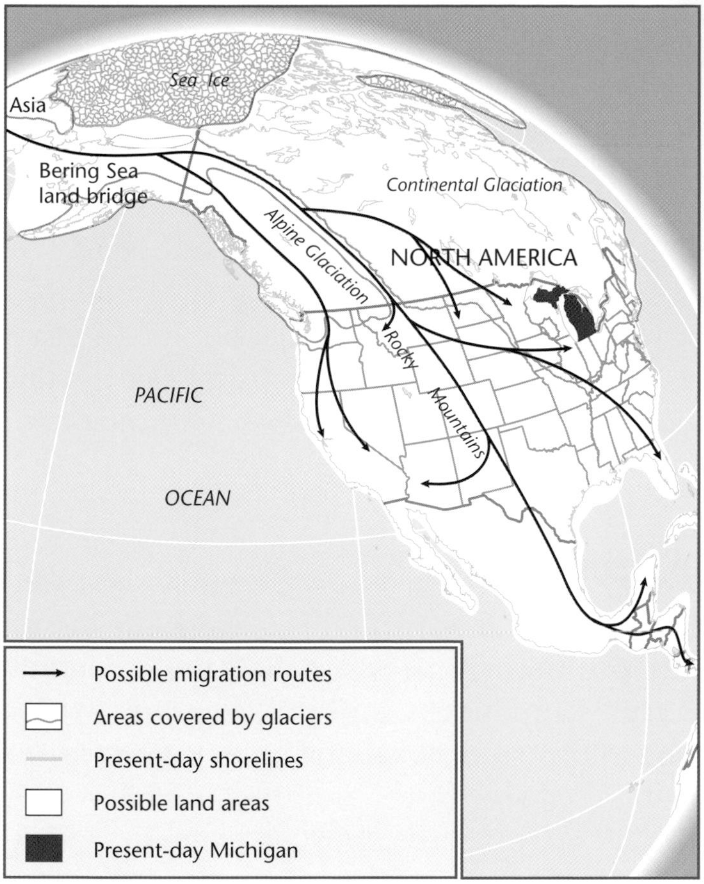

Sea Ice
Asia
Bering Sea land bridge
Continental Glaciation
Alpine Glaciation
NORTH AMERICA
Rocky Mountains
PACIFIC
OCEAN
Possible migration routes
Areas covered by glaciers
Present-day shorelines
Possible land areas
Present-day Michigan

Most Native Americans believe their people have always been in the Americas. Evidence suggests that Paleo-Indians probably came from Asia, across the Bering Sea land bridge.

Paleo-Indians

As time passed, the **climate** began to change. Warmer temperatures allowed new plants and trees to grow. This new vegetation provided food for the Paleo-Indians, the name **archaeologists** gave to these early prehistoric nomads. The Paleo-Indians were also called hunters and gatherers because they hunted animals and gathered berries and nuts for food. The giant mastodon and caribou, covered in cold-weather fur, fled to colder spots north in Canada as the summers became too warm for them. The Paleo-Indians eventually disappeared as well, perhaps because the changing climate made food scarce, or because they followed the animals to a cooler climate.

Archaic Peoples in Michigan

New groups came to the area. Archaeologists called these groups the Archaic Peoples. The way these people lived, their beliefs, and their belongings, are mysteries, but their tools and weapons explain part of the story.

The Old Copper Indians were a group of Archaic Native Americans who lived in the area that would become Michigan. They lived on Isle Royale, an island in northern Lake Superior. They mined copper, which they used on their weapons. Copper was also found on other **artifacts** left behind by this tribe. Scientists say the Old Copper Indians also invented the birch–bark canoe used later by many tribes.

WOODLAND PEOPLE

The Archaic Period ended about 1000 C.E. with the arrival of yet another **prehistoric** people called the Woodland People. This highly productive and skillful group settled throughout the Midwest. A Woodland tribe known as the Hopewell Indians were called moundbuilders. They built mounds for ceremonies, burials, and to use as sundials to tell the seasons.

Woodland tribes also carved **petroglyphs.** The Sanilac Petroglyphs, in the Sanilac Petroglyphs **Historic** State Park in Bad Axe, are still visible today. Historians think the designs, etched in the soft sandstone by hand, are 300 to 1,000 years old.

Scientists determined that the region was still cold when mammoths lived because those animals could not live in warm **climates.**

ANISHINAABEK: FIRST PEOPLE IN OJIBWAY

Historic Native Americans met early European explorers in the mid-1600s. Three of these historic tribes joined together to form an **alliance.** They called themselves the Anishinaabek, which means "first people" in Ojibway. They **migrated** from the east coast.

The petroglyphs were first discovered after huge forest fires burned the Lower Peninsula in 1881.

These three tribes, the Ojibway, also called Chippewa by the French, the Ottawa, and the Potawatomi, spoke a similar language and called themselves brothers. The Ojibway were the "older brothers," next were the Ottawa, and the Potawatomi were the "younger brothers." They were called the People of the Three Fires because of their agreement to support each other. The Anishinaabek were generous people, giving gifts and help to those who needed it.

The Potawatomi tribes became excellent farmers and lived in permanent settlements in the southern portion of the Lower Peninsula. The Ojibway were hunters and fishers who lived along southern Lake Superior. The Ottawa were known as traders and builders of birch–bark canoes. They lived along the shores of Lake Michigan. Members of these tribes still live in Michigan today.

HURON

The Huron lived in the Georgian Bay region of Lake Huron in Canada. The Huron were known as skilled fur traders. However, they had to compete with the powerful Iroquois Nation that also traded furs in the area. The competition between the two groups resulted in the Huron being run off their land in Canada. They

Although the Sauk and Fox had separate tribal chiefs, the United States considers them to be one tribe, called "the Sauk and Fox."

settled in Michigan. They were the region's largest tribe, perhaps because they lived in villages and did not move often. The women were excellent gardeners and the men fished in nearby lakes and streams.

MENOMINEE

The Menominee lived in the Upper Peninsula, near several bodies of water. The water was an important source of food for this tribe. The name *Menominee* means "wild rice people." They harvested wild rice from the shallow waters and ate the sturgeon they caught. They also were hunters and gatherers.

SAUK, FOX, AND MIAMI

Various smaller tribes, such as the Sauk, Fox, and Miami, also lived in Michigan. The Sauk, also spelled Sac, and the Fox formed an **alliance** and sometimes were even mistaken as one tribe. One of their early trails, called the Great Sauk Trail, became famous as the path these and other Native Americans took across southern Michigan. Eventually, this trail led out of the state and further west as tribes were pushed further west and south.

The Miami lived in the Wisconsin area before moving south to the end of Lake Michigan near the present-day border with Indiana and Illinois. The name *Miami* may come from the word *oumamik*, which means "people of the peninsula." The Miami were known to be excellent farmers and went buffalo hunting once a year. They moved to Ohio during the 1700s.

Tribes of Michigan, 1763

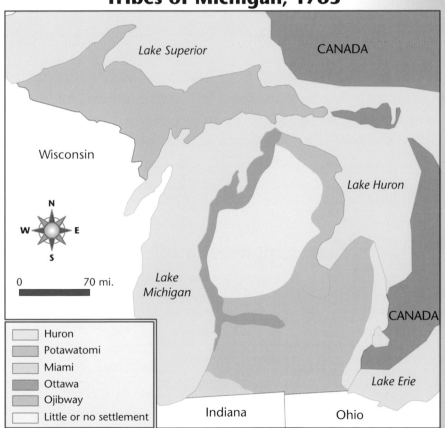

Michigan's native peoples settled in many areas around the state. They especially liked to live in areas near water because it provided food and transportation.

Explorers and Native Americans in Michigan, 1585-1763

In about 1618, Étienne Brulé became the first European to discover the area that is now Michigan. He had been sent by Samuel de Champlain, another French explorer, to find the Northwest Passage, a supposed shortcut to China. In 1634, Jean Nicolet, also sent by Champlain, passed through the Straits of Mackinac and explored the southern shore of the Upper Peninsula.

Early Explorers in Michigan

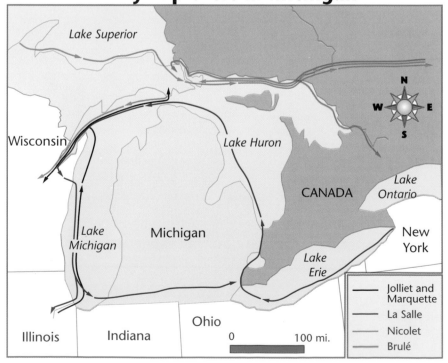

MISSIONS

Early explorers, expecting to find new routes to Asia, often traveled with the "black robes," the name Native Americans gave to **missionaries.** Missionaries came to teach their religion to those they met. They built **missions** to teach **Catholicism,** but the Native Americans had their own beliefs and were not willing to give them up.

One of Michigan's most famous missionaries was Father Jacques Marquette. He helped build missions at Sault Ste. Marie and the Straits of Mackinac. He became the first Frenchman to explore the Mississippi River. Beginning at St. Ignace, he and explorer Louis Jolliet traced rivers all the way to the Mississippi River. As they traveled the Mississippi, they thought they were discovering the shortcut to Asia. When they realized they were headed south to the Gulf of Mexico, however, they came back.

FUR TRADING

The Native Americans were eager to trade with the French fur traders and soon became used to European products—guns and other weapons, blankets, and whiskey. Bear, muskrat, mink, wolf, fox, and other animal furs were trapped and traded, but beaver pelts were the most valuable. The furs became hats, muffs, and coats for the wealthy people in Europe. As a result of over-hunting, the beaver popula-tion was nearly wiped out.

Jacques Marquette and Louis Jolliet brought Native Americans with them on their trip down the Mississippi River.

A Fur Trader's Life

Legends tell of the fur traders' lives. They were also called *voyageurs* (pronounced voy-a-jurs). They showed their great strength and their ability to paddle their heavy canoes for hours. Some stories say that French voyageurs could paddle 100 miles a day. Their canoes were loaded with animal pelts, but they nearly raced to reach the trading posts. They carried both their canoes and their furs when they moved over land.

There were an estimated ten million beavers living in the Great Lakes region when the Europeans arrived, but by the end of the 1600s, beavers were rare around the Straits of Mackinac.

As Native Americans moved to better hunting grounds within the area, traders followed. French fur traders and explorers such as René Robert Cavelier, Sieur de la Salle set up outposts along routes to make trading easier to control. They set up a string of **forts** to protect their trade. Among them were forts at the St. Joseph River, Sault Ste. Marie, and the Straits of Mackinac. The towns of St. Ignace and Mackinaw City grew from the trading posts located near the forts.

Antoine de la Mothe Cadillac created the last French fort in the Michigan area in 1701. It was called Fort Ponchartrain du De Troit. This fort became what is now the city of Detroit. Detroit's early settlers came from Canada with Cadillac.

French fur traders and **missionaries** got along well with the Native Americans, despite their **cultural** differences. Fur trading with the Native Americans was

Cadillac and his men reached the Detroit River on July 23, 1701. The following day, the group traveled north on the Detroit River and chose a place to build the new settlement that would eventually become Detroit.

important to the economy in the 1600s and 1700s. However, the French and British began fighting in the colonies over who would control trade with the Native Americans.

FRENCH AND INDIAN WAR

The war in the colonies that began in 1754 was called the French and Indian War because most of the Native Americans sided with the French explorers. In 1756, France and Britain began fighting on their homelands in Europe as well. The European war was called the Seven Years' War.

No battles during the French and Indian War were fought in Michigan. However, the French and Native

Americans from Michigan fought the British in battles as far east as Quebec, Canada. Both the French and Indian War and the Seven Years' War ended in 1763 with the French losing all claims to land and water in the colonies. They signed the Treaty of Paris, giving everything to the British.

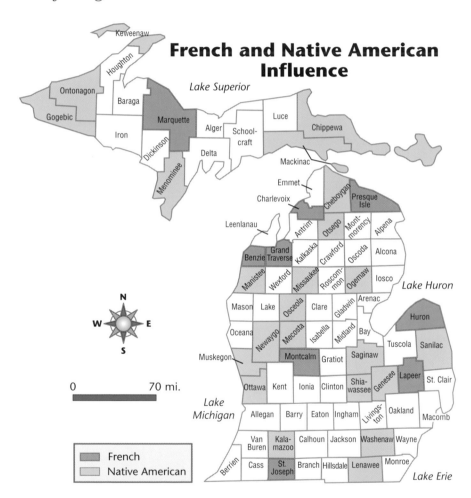

French and Native American Influence

Even after they were defeated, the French remained throughout the Great Lakes region. The early French and Native American heritage still shines throughout what is now Michigan. A map of Michigan reveals the influence of the French and Native Americans in its county names.

Revolution and the New Nation, 1763-1815

After the French and Indian War, the British promised the Native Americans fair treatment, continued fur trade, and gifts like the French supplied. However, the British did not keep their promises. They refused to supply Native Americans with guns, weapons, and **ammunition.**

THE BRITISH IN MICHIGAN

The Native Americans in Michigan and throughout the Ohio Valley worried about the American colonists moving west and settling on their hunting grounds. During the French and Indian War, Ottawa Chief Pontiac had made an agreement with British troops to treat each other with respect, but he soon realized that would not happen. Native Americans were being pushed off their land by people looking for land to live on.

In 1763, Pontiac tried to organize the tribes and capture the British at **Fort** Detroit. He hoped the French would help. Native American tribes near Fort Pitt, Fort Niagara, and Fort Michilimackinac planned similar attacks. The Native Americans were successful in capturing all the Michigan forts, except for one. The British defeated Chief Pontiac at Fort Detroit. After the French failed to help his warriors, Pontiac and the tribes that joined him retreated and returned to their settlements.

Some say these attacks, called Pontiac's **Rebellion,** began the unrest leading up to the American Revolution

During his life, Chief Pontiac was well known throughout Michigan. Today, many places in Michigan, including the city of Pontiac, are named after him.

• •

(1775–1783). Pontiac's **Rebellion** brought increased anti-British feelings among Native Americans. In response, Britain sent 120,000 troops to the colonies to maintain control and set limits to **migration** into the western lands. Britain also set higher taxes and stricter controls on Americans in the colonies.

THE REVOLUTIONARY WAR

Britain thought the Proclamation of 1763, which reserved all lands west of the Alleghenies for the Native Americans, would help resolve Native American uprising and protect the fur trade. Instead, it angered colonists that held western land claims. The colonists decided that fighting for their independence would be the best thing to do. The Revolutionary War between the colonies and Britain began in 1775.

No Revolutionary War battles were fought on the land that would become Michigan, but the British did still control **Fort** Detroit. This fort served as headquarters for their troops. In 1781, the British abandoned the post and moved to Fort Mackinac on Mackinac Island.

The victory of the colonists in the Revolutionary War brought many changes to the Midwest area. One question was where to place the border between the United States and Canada. After several proposals, the British decided on a boundary that put a line down the middle of four of the five Great Lakes. Those boundaries are still in effect today. Of the five Great Lakes, only Lake Michigan is entirely within the United States.

Refusing to Leave

When the Revolutionary War ended in 1783, Michigan should have been under the new government's rules, but the British refused to leave. They stayed until September 1, 1796 when the red, white, and blue American flag finally flew over Fort Michilimackinac on Mackinac Island and Fort Detroit.

A NEW NATION

After the Revolutionary War, the American colonies were joined together as a new nation, the United States of America. The new U.S. **Congress** passed several **ordinances** as a way to bring order to the new nation. In 1787, the Northwest Ordinance was written. The ordinance described boundaries for the Northwest Territory, land that was not yet divided into states. This land was east of the Mississippi River and north of the Ohio River to the Great Lakes. The future states of Michigan, Indiana, Ohio, Illinois, and Wisconsin were part of this region. The ordinance stated that there would be no slavery in this region and that part of the land would be set aside for building schools. A fair and orderly method of dividing the territory into states and steps toward achieving statehood and self-government were also outlined.

This building is a reconstruction of Fort Michilimackinac. It is part of Michilimackinac State Park in Mackinaw City.

Michigan and the Northwest Territory

Americans named this area the Northwest Territory because at that time, it was the northwestern portion of the newly independent United States. No one had explored further west yet.

The first state to be carved out of the Northwest Territory was Ohio. It became a state in 1803. In 1805, Michigan became a separate territory. This territory included the Lower Peninsula and part of the Upper Peninsula. Detroit became the first **capital** of the territory and William Hull served as governor.

TROUBLE IN MICHIGAN TERRITORY

Although the Michigan Territory was established, traveling to the area was difficult. New settlers stayed away in fear of Native American **rebellions** over losing their land. Native Americans were trying to make peace with the settlers, but they also wanted to keep their lands. With each new group of pioneers who came to clear the land and set up homes, Native Americans were crowded in their space or pushed out altogether.

Settlement had just begun when Michigan found itself involved in the War of 1812. The British tried again to take **Fort** Mackinac and Detroit. Battles were fought around Detroit and in Lake Erie. Governor William Hull became General Hull when fighting reached the Michigan Territory. Tecumseh, the famous Shawnee chief, traveled north from Ohio and sided with the British during the War of 1812.

Tecumseh fooled General Hull into thinking that thousands of his warriors were ready to attack the fort. Afraid that he could not win, General Hull surrendered Detroit to the British without having a battle. Because of his cowardly decision, Hull was convicted of **treason.** The penalty was death, but he was spared because of his brave leadership during the Revolutionary War (1775–1783). Hull left Michigan and moved back to his hometown in Massachusetts.

Tecumseh and his supporters moved south to the Ohio region, where they fought at Fort Meigs. On October 5, 1813, Tecumseh was killed near the Thames River in Ontario, Canada. The United States regained Michigan from the British, including the Upper Peninsula and the lakes surrounding it. The Treaty of Ghent was signed in 1814, ending the War of 1812. Once the war was over, the next governor of the Michigan Territory, Lewis Cass, had an important task. He wanted settlers to build communities so that Michigan could become a state.

Judge Augustus Woodward

Soon after Detroit became the state capital, a fire burned everything but the fort and buildings further down the Detroit River. U.S. president Thomas Jefferson sent several men, including Judge Augustus Woodward, to govern and rebuild Detroit. Reminders of these men still exist in Detroit today. Woodward named a main street for himself and other streets for his friends, such as Jefferson, Monroe, and Madison.

Building Roads to Statehood, 1816–1849

Building roads were important to Governor Cass's plan of increasing the territory's population. The roads were more like paths in early days, similar to hiking paths we know today. During the War of 1812, a few of the trails were widened by American soldiers, but they were still very difficult to travel.

Governor Cass also knew the Great Lakes, especially Lake Erie, were difficult to travel safely. Shipwrecks were common. He needed to improve transportation, both on the Great Lakes and on land to attract settlers. Building lighthouses to mark hazardous spots was one way to make sailing the Great Lakes safer. 124 lighthouses eventually lit the way for captains sailing ships on the Great Lakes.

Luckily for Governor Cass, a new route for transportation would soon make getting to Michigan much easier. In 1825, the first U.S. canal, called the Erie Canal, opened. It provided transportation between Albany and Buffalo, New York. From Buffalo, settlers could take overland roadways or boats through Lake Erie to reach Detroit. The first highway in the Michigan Territory, called the Chicago Road—still an important highway today—made the biggest difference in land transportation. Once transportation improved, settlers were eager to travel west to Michigan. Land was cheaper in the Michigan Territory than in crowded eastern states. By the 1830s, settlers began discovering

Michigan Lighthouses

Lake Superior

Marquette

Sault Ste. Marie

N
W   E
S

Traverse City

Lake Huron

0   70 mi.

Bay City

Port Huron

Lansing

Lake Michigan

Kalamazoo

Detroit

Lake Erie

While many of Michigan's lighthouses are still in use today, many others are used as summer homes, museums, and park exhibits.

the farmland of the Lower Peninsula. Pioneers also came for the plentiful timber for building and heating. The population grew to over 212,000 after the Erie Canal linked eastern cities like New York and Buffalo with Michigan settlements.

ORDINANCE OF 1787

The **Ordinance** of 1787 stated that 60,000 white male residents were needed before a state **constitution** could be adopted. A **census** in 1835 showed that Michigan met the requirement. There was one problem that delayed Michigan's statehood, though. Both Ohio and Michigan claimed an area called the Toledo Strip. In 1837, a nonviolent war, called the Toledo War, took place between

Part of the Maumee River at Toledo on Lake Erie was fought over in the 1835 war between Ohio and the Michigan Territory.

Ohioans and Michiganians over a small strip of land bordering the Maumee River. No gunshots were ever fired. After two years of arguing, **delegates** from both sides met at a special convention in Ann Arbor, and they reached a compromise. U.S. president Andrew Jackson gave Toledo to Ohio, and Michigan was awarded an additional 9,000 acres in the Upper Peninsula in 1836. At the time, most Michiganians were not happy with the outcome, but they settled so Michigan could become a state. Later, when they found the Upper Peninsula rich in **minerals,** they were much happier. On January 26, 1837, Michigan became the 26th state.

THE STATE CAPITAL

The state **capital** remained in Detroit until state **legislators** voted to move it to a more central location in Lansing in 1847. Michigan's state **capitol** building, located in the Capitol Complex in downtown Lansing, reminds visitors of the U.S. Capitol in Washington, D.C. The **architect** of the state building, Elijah E. Meyers, designed it with a large round dome. Like the U.S.

During the late 1980s and early 1990s, workers spent five years restoring the Capitol to its original beauty. The renovation was completed in 1992.

Capitol in Washington, D.C., it stands out, towering above the nearby buildings. Michigan's capitol was first completed in 1879.

Between the time Michigan became a state and the permanent capitol was completed, many other events changed Michigan. Just after the canals opened in the late 1820s, railroads began bringing thousands more people to Michigan. The state was growing in population. People came to farm, but they also heard of new **industries** in Michigan. The Upper Peninsula turned out to be a gold mine—or so some settlers thought. They found "fool's gold," or pyrite, which is a **mineral** that looks like gold. True gold miners, in search of real gold, did not stay. They left for settlements out west in California. Other miners stayed in Michigan for the copper, coal, and iron **ore.**

SETTLING THE LAND

More settlers came to Michigan from New York than any other state. **Immigrants** from Europe heard about the opportunities in Michigan and eagerly left for the new state, too. Settlers who did not want to farm or mine came because of the lumber industry. The lumber camps and mill towns attracted **immigrants** from

Governor Stevens T. Mason

Stevens T. Mason served as secretary of the Michigan Territory at age 19. He became the acting governor of the territory and then Michigan's first governor when he was 23 years old. He was nicknamed "Boy Governor" because of his very young age.

countries like Norway and Sweden. People from Denmark preferred the **fertile** farmland. Dutch settlements sprang up in the Lower Peninsula. They settled near Lake Michigan in 1845 and named their town Holland, after their homeland.

Pioneer life was hard. It was probably more difficult than most families expected at the time. Families had to rely on themselves for food and shelter. They cut down the trees with axes and built log cabins. Necessary building tools such as nails were scarce or unavailable. The settlers quickly cleared land to plant crops for their families. Often, wild animals ate the crops and livestock, leaving owners to start over.

Even with these hardships, early settlers valued education and built schools. The federal government provided land to raise money for schools. The plan was outlined in the territory **ordinance.** It provided a piece of land in each township for building or purchasing land for a school. Each township had one parcel, called Section 16, set aside for schools.

Lumbering was dangerous and tiring work. People worked for months at a time, only getting Sundays off.

Civil War and Reconstruction, 1850–1865

By the mid-1800s, Michiganians, like the rest of the country, focused on the national problem of slavery. Quakers and other religions set up **abolition** societies. The first society in Michigan began in Lenawee County in 1832. Abolitionists believed slavery was wrong and wanted to end it. They held meetings to plan ways to secretly help slaves escape to Canada. Michigan was a free state, but some people living there owned slaves they brought when they moved from the South.

Crosswhite Family

One of the most famous Michigan slave stories began in Marshall, east of Battle Creek. Here a slave family, the Crosswhites, escaped from Kentucky and got as far as this southern Michigan town. That's where their owners caught up with them, but the citizens of Marshall refused to let the Kentuckians leave with the Crosswhites. In the end, the people of Marshall were fined. They paid a sum equal to what the Crosswhites would have been sold for at a slave auction. Some historians believe that Adam Crosswhite and the story of his family in Marshall became characters in a famous book, *Uncle Tom's Cabin*. The author, Harriet Beecher Stowe, wrote her book about slavery before the Civil War.

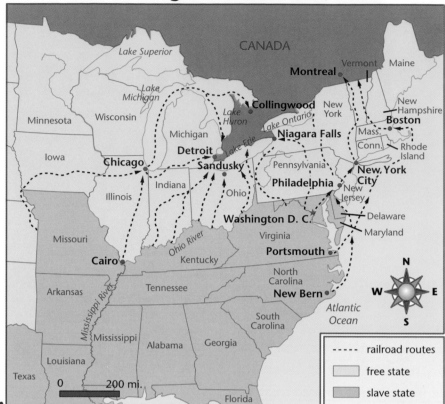

The Underground Railroad, 1860

The Underground Railroad was the passage to freedom for slaves. Its secret routes wound throughout the Midwest toward Detroit, which was known as "Midnight" by those seeking safety.

MICHIGAN'S LINK TO SLAVERY

From 1850 to 1860, arguments over slavery grew worse throughout the United States. The Compromise of 1850 was supposed to help settle land arguments out West and lessen the slavery issue. The Compromise included the Fugitive Slave Act of 1850, which made it illegal to help runaway slaves. This law made it more difficult for escaping slaves to find freedom in the North. Because of these new laws, **abolitionists** worked even harder to set up the Underground Railroad, a network of secret routes. They planned escape routes to link slaves up with other abolitionists further along the secret route to freedom. Usually, slaves went through Battle Creek or Adrian to reach Detroit. From Detroit they fled by boat to freedom in Canada.

UNDERGROUND RAILROAD LEADERS

Michigan had some brave people who were leaders in creating and running the Underground Railroad. Sojourner Truth, an African-American abolitionist, lived in Battle Creek. She was born into slavery in New York state and named Isabella Baumfree. Once she was free, she changed her name and began speaking out against slavery and for women's rights. She spoke publicly about her life as a slave and helped other slaves when they gained freedom. Her "Ain't I a Woman" speech became famous when she began speaking out for women's rights. A monument of Sojourner Truth stands in Battle Creek at Linear Park.

Laura Smith Haviland helped so many slaves escape through Adrian that Southern **bounty hunters** put out a reward for her capture. Some people believe she helped 1,000 slaves escape. Her home and her husband's barn were among Michigan's first stops along the Underground Railroad. After the Fugitive Slave Act was passed, she worked openly, not in secret like other underground railroad conductors. When the Civil War began, she continued to help by delivering supplies and helping war victims.

MORE UNREST

Abolitionists were angered when **Congress** passed another law, the Kansas-Nebraska Act of 1854. It said that settlers in new territories could vote on whether or not they wanted slaves. This law went against the Northwest **Ordinance** of 1787 that said no states carved from the Northwest Territory would have slaves. Northerners, especially the ones from the Northwest Territory, like Michigan, disagreed with this new act.

*Sojourner Truth was the first African-American woman to play a large part in the **women's rights movement.***

Laura Smith Haviland began a school in Adrian, called the Raisin Institute, for both black and white children.

This newspaper ran a front page story about the Dred Scott decision in 1857. The story included illustrations of Scott and his family.

In 1857, the Supreme Court heard the Dred Scott Case. Dred Scott was a slave living in Illinois, a free state. His case had to do with whether moving a slave from a state that allowed slavery to a free state meant that person was still a slave. Scott tried to gain his freedom by taking his case to court. The Supreme Court ruled that slaves were not citizens and their owners could move them along with other property when they moved to a free state. This decision moved the country one step closer to a civil war.

U.S. president Abraham Lincoln promised in his **inaugural address** to "preserve, protect, and defend" the United States, but the states were not united. They were divided in their feelings about slavery. The Southern states wanted slaves to work on their plantations and harvest their cotton fields. Most people in the North did not want slavery to continue. But even though most northerners did not have slaves, many Northerners did not treat African Americans fairly. African Americans were not counted in the **census.** They could not vote. Their children could not attend white schools.

Tensions over slavery grew between the North and the South. Questions about allowing slavery in western states and Supreme Court decisions made both sides angry. Debates about slavery and Harriet B. Stowe's book, *Uncle Tom's Cabin,* put the topic of slavery in everyone's conversations. After President Lincoln was elected in 1861, the Southern states formed the Confederate States of America. This led to the Civil War.

THE CIVIL WAR (1861-1865)

The Civil War began April 12, 1861, at the Battle of **Fort** Sumter. The Northern troops were the Union. The Southerners joined the Confederates. Sometimes family members fought against each other, depending upon where they lived. President Lincoln called for Union volunteers. He did not want Southern states to leave the Union, but he strongly opposed slavery. He thought it was his duty as president to protect the **Constitution.**

These men were officers and enlisted men of the 4th Michigan Infantry Unit during the Civil War.

The First Michigan Infantry was the first military unit from the western states to arrive in Washington, D.C. About 90,000 Michiganians signed up and marched off to war. That was nearly one person out of every four who lived in Michigan. Michigan Union soldiers took part in more than 800 battles during the Civil War. Sadly, one out of six of them were killed. Black soldiers were **segregated** because of their race. Michigan's black soldiers fought in the 102nd United States Colored Infantry Regiment.

CIVIL WAR GENERALS

Several Civil War generals came from Michigan, but George Armstrong Custer may have been the most famous. He led his Michigan troops into many major battles, including the Battle at Gettysburg in Pennsylvania. Michigan's 24th Infantry fought under

General Custer

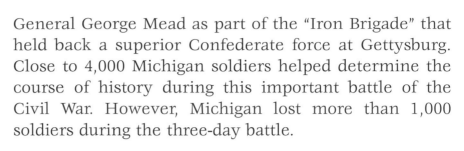

General George Mead as part of the "Iron Brigade" that held back a superior Confederate force at Gettysburg. Close to 4,000 Michigan soldiers helped determine the course of history during this important battle of the Civil War. However, Michigan lost more than 1,000 soldiers during the three-day battle.

THE WOMEN'S ROLE

During the Civil War, some women took over men's jobs at home. They often nursed the injured in makeshift or temporary hospitals close to battlefields. Annie Etheridge volunteered as a nurse and traveled with Michigan units. The injured called her Michigan Annie and Gentle Annie.

Annie Etheridge was awarded the Kearny Cross of Honor for her bravery.

Other women served on the battlefield, but the only Michigan female known for certain to take part in the fighting was Sarah Emma Edmonds. She joined the army as a man named Frank Thompson. She fought in several major battles, served as an aide to Colonel Orlando M. Poe, and completed missions behind Confederate lines disguised as a woman. She was accused of **deserting** the army in April 1863, but was actually in a hospital, recovering from malaria. Edmonds received an **honorable discharge** in 1884.

The Civil War ended after the Union captured the Confederate **capital** in Richmond, Virginia in 1865. Celebrations and parades were held throughout Michigan. It would take several more years for national lawmakers to reunite the Northern and Southern states. Unfortunately, President Lincoln could not help. He was **assassinated** just five days after the Southern troops surrendered.

Michigan's Industrial Growth, 1866-1918

During the Civil War, those who stayed behind at home worked hard to supply the troops with necessary war supplies. When soldiers returned, they were eager to go back to work. There was no better place than in the lumber **industry.** Settlers were moving farther west and needed wood for homes and fuel. The lumber states of Maine and New York, where easterners obtained their supplies, were running low. The forests of Michigan, full of the white pine builders favored, became the center of lumbering in the United States by 1869.

THE LEADER IN LOGGING

There were enough trees to keep Michigan leading the logging industry for over fifty years. Michigan hit a lumber production record in 1889 when 5.5 billion **board feet** of lumber was produced.

This illustration from 1886 shows a train carrying pine logs. Michigan's white pine trees became lumber for homes, railroad ties, wooden pails, and toothpicks during the 1880s.

Loggers holding sharp poles are standing on a log jam, waiting to transport the logs downstream.

The only way to get huge logs to mills and markets in the days before railroads was to float them on Michigan rivers. This process was called booming. To get the pine logs to the rivers, loggers worked all winter, piling the logs on long bobsleds. They slid them down snow-covered roads to the frozen streams and waited for the spring thaw. Mills opened each spring to slice the logs into timber for Michigan's lumber-related factories.

New inventions, like steam-powered saws, replaced slower methods. Lumber was ready for market faster. Silas Overback invented a way to log in the winter when there was no snow for the sleds usually used to get lumber to the rivers. He used huge wheels, called Big Wheels because of their size, to support horse-drawn wagons. Logging railroads were invented soon after. Loggers could work year-round and they could move lumber greater distances from the mills. Loggers could also cut down hardwood trees, such as hickory, maple, and ash, that were too heavy to float down the rivers.

Loggers lived in temporary villages or camps called shanties. Logging companies in charge of cutting down the trees and moving them to the sawmills owned the camps. Lumberers came to work there from other southern Michigan areas and other states. Word of the jobs even spread across the Atlantic Ocean. Soon, **immigrants** from England, Sweden, Norway, Ireland, and Finland came to Michigan to work in the rugged camps.

EXPANDING TRANSPORTATION

The Great Lakes provided a great water-way, but the rapids at St. Mary's River prevented **barges** from passing between Lake Superior and Lake Huron. Native Americans carried their canoes to avoid the 20-foot rapids of Lake Superior dumping into Lake Huron. Something had to be done to make this area safe for transportation. In 1855, the first barge passed through the Soo **Locks.** The locks system makes the uneven depths of the two bodies of water the same by opening and closing gates at either end of the lock. The Soo Locks at Sault Ste. Marie are the busiest in the world. From the 1880s through the beginning of the 1900s, iron mines opened across the Upper Peninsula. Huge barges carried the **ore** to markets in nearby states and far away.

As people moved into the area, towns grew into cities and Michigan became an **industrial** center. Organizations, such as the Western Federation of Miners and the American Federation of Labor, helped miners get higher pay and safer working conditions. Michigan's inventors and businesspeople, using the state's resources, were leading the country in manufacturing.

MAKING FURNITURE

While logging and mining industries thrived, businesspeople were building factories. One industry that began as a result of logging was furniture making. Grand Rapids, located on the western side of the Lower Peninsula, became the Furniture Capital of the World.

Before the Soo Locks were built, people sailing to Michigan had to unload their boats, haul the cargo around the rapids in wagons, and reload in other boats on the other side.

Charles C. Comstock was a lumberer from New Hampshire. He moved to Michigan and started the first furniture factory in Grand Rapids, The Grand Rapids Chair Company, in 1862.

Train service increased and manufacturers could transport their products more easily. Also, a time-saving machine, the dry kiln, was invented by A. D. Linn and Z. Clark Thwing. It was a dryer to speed the drying of sap from the wood. Prior to this invention, wood took up to four years to dry before it could be manufactured into high quality furniture. Soon, other cities in Michigan, including Detroit, Holland, and Monroe, opened furniture factories, too.

AUTOMOBILE INDUSTRY

Charles B. King and Henry Ford manufactured the first automobiles in Detroit. Historians think King may have been the first to drive a gas-powered auto the evening of March 6, 1896, several months before Henry Ford's model

Henry Ford's quadricycle had four wire wheels that looked like heavy bicycle wheels, was steered with a tiller like a boat, and had only two forward speeds with no reverse.

was tested. Other inventors, like Ransom Olds, Alexander Winton, and Charles and Frank Duryea had also built motorized vehicles. Then Henry Ford drove a quadricycle he built in June. Ransom E. Olds, who lived in Lansing, tested his gasoline engine on August 11, 1896.

The first production Model T Ford was assembled at the Piquette Avenue Plant in Detroit on October 1, 1908.

In 1908, Henry Ford's first Model T cars were a huge success. They cost $850 when they came out, making the cars affordable for American families. The Model T was not fancy. It only came in black. By 1913, the Ford Motor Company's Model T was so popular that faster production was necessary to keep up with demand for the car. The assembly line method of construction reduced production time from 12.5 hours to 1.5 hours per car. Workers from **rural** areas **migrated** to the cities for jobs in the automobile factories.

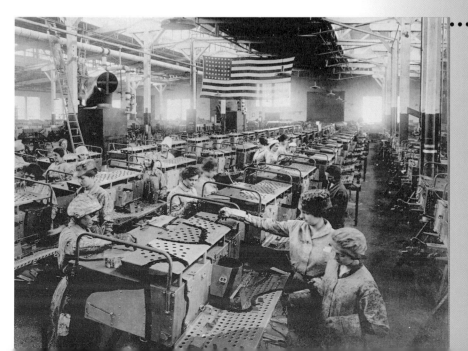

During World War I, female factory workers painted military vehicle parts at the American Car & Foundry Company in Detroit.

Home of Breakfast Cereal

Some industries sprang up in Michigan that had nothing to do with mining or logging. William Keith Kellogg accidentally invented corn flakes, a breakfast cereal. He helped his brother, Dr. John Harvey Kellogg at the Battle Creek Sanitorium, a hospital where people came to learn how to live healthier. Dr. Kellogg was experimenting with making an easy-to-digest health food. Together, the brothers created cereal flakes made from many grains.

In 1891, Charles W. Post came to Dr. Kellogg's hospital as a patient, but after eating the cereal, he stayed in Battle Creek and created his own breakfast foods, such as Postum and Grape-Nuts. Post and the Kelloggs made cereal a household word and a full aisle in the grocery store. Battle Creek is still called Cereal City today.

WORLD WAR I (1914–1918)

The auto **industry** in the United States boomed in the early 1900s, but across the Atlantic Ocean, problems in Europe led to World War I. On April 6, 1917, the United States and the **Allies** went to war with Germany. Michigan, like other states, participated in federal programs to provide for war costs. Michiganians also produced airplane engines, trucks, and tanks in factories that normally manufactured auto parts. The Ford Motor Company created a new company to build submarines.

With the start of World War I, Michigan needed thousands of workers to build factories and work on their production lines. Polish people made up the largest group of new **immigrants** eager to work in the auto plants. Other groups from Yugoslavia, Romania, and the Middle East added to the **cultural diversity** in Michigan during this increase in immigration.

The Great Depression and World War II, 1929-1945

After World War I, Michigan employees felt well-off and successful. More than 5,000,000 cars were sold by 1929. Workers and their families continued to spend their high wages. People borrowed money for purchases they could not afford. Eventually, Michigan factory workers, as well as everyone else in the United States, fell upon hard times. The United States' economy failed. Then the stock market crashed in October of 1929. Banks closed. Companies could not pay their employees. Few cars were sold. All of these conditions caused an economic **depression** throughout the United States, including Michigan. It was called the Great Depression.

When Franklin D. Roosevelt was elected as 32nd president of the United States, he developed a plan called the New Deal. To pay unemployed workers, he set up public works agencies. Young men in the Civilian Conservation Corps, called the CCC for short, worked to **conserve** nature. They built state and national forests and parks. They planted 484 million trees in Michigan alone. The lumber industry had stripped the forests, but CCC workers reforested many of the areas left empty by the logging industry. They fought forest fires and built dams, bridges, and buildings. Many artists and writers

These men were part of the Civil Conservation Corps. They worked as loggers in Michigan in 1934.

were also unemployed. They received jobs with the Works Progress Administration, known as the WPA. They painted murals in public buildings and took on other creative projects.

IMPROVING WORKING CONDITIONS

As factory workers gradually found jobs again, they discovered working conditions worse than before the **depression.** As a result, **industrial** trade **unions** formed in Michigan. The autoworkers formed the Automobile Workers of America (UAW) in 1935 to gain safer and better working conditions. In 1936, workers at the Flint General Motors plant participated in a sit-down strike. It would be the first of many strikes, but it unified workers in other factories who soon joined or formed unions.

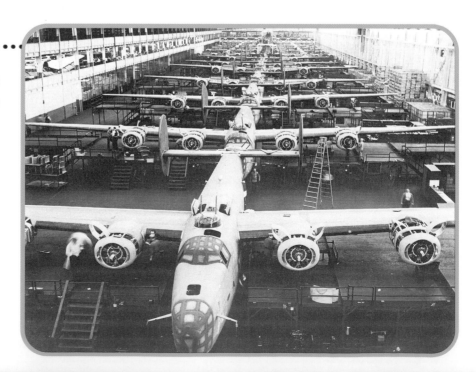

Huge B-24 bombers were built at Henry Ford's Willow Run plant in Detroit.

There were huge campaigns of posters and flyers that went around the country, supporting the idea of women entering the workplace while men were away in the war. A "Rosie the Riveter" song was also written to encourage women's involvement in the workforce.

WORLD WAR II (1939–1945)

The United States entered World War II after Pearl Harbor was attacked on December 7, 1941. Unlike World War I, this time Michigan plants stopped building cars for Americans. Factories turned their usual production lines into war product lines, building tanks, guns, aircraft, and **ammunition.** Near Ypsilanti, the Ford Motor Company built the Willow Run Bomber Plant to make B-24 bombers. It was the largest **assembly plant** ever built.

Before WWII, most women did not work outside the home. The war effort changed that for Michigan women. They took the factory jobs left by men joining the military. About 200,000 women worked in Michigan factories, building the necessary wartime equipment. Women who worked in factories earned a new national nickname and a strong new image. They were nicknamed Rosie the Riveter. Millions of "Rosies" did the same job men did before the war. These "Rosies" began the **women's rights movement.**

Modern Michigan, 1946–Today

After World War II, Michigan factories went back to making cars. Returning soldiers and their young families wanted new cars. It took about four years to build all the cars buyers were waiting for. The post-war years were marked by the desire to have fun and enjoy life.

G. Mennen Williams was elected governor of Michigan in 1948. He served six two-year terms, from 1949 through 1960. While he was governor, he worked on approving the building of the five-mile long Mackinac Bridge. It connected the Upper and Lower Peninsulas, and opened in 1957. Just a year before, in 1956, the federal highway act provided 90 percent of the funding necessary to build toll-free highways across the United States. In Michigan these roads included I-96, I-75, and I-69. These superhighways made travel between states and within Michigan easier and faster.

G. Mennen Williams

Governor Williams's nickname was "Soapy" because his very wealthy family owned the Mennen Company, a company that manufactured toiletries, soaps, and other products. They were packaged in green and white wrappers. In tribute to his family, Governor Williams always wore a green and white bow tie.

The Big Mac, as the Mackinac Bridge is often called, is one of Michigan's best-known attractions.

CIVIL RIGHTS MOVEMENT

The Civil Rights movement began in the United States in the mid-1950s when the U.S. Supreme Court ruled that school **segregation** was against the **Constitution.** The decade following this landmark decision resulted in heated debates, marches, and demonstrations. Sometimes the demonstrations were peaceful gatherings and other times, **riots** broke out. The city of Detroit invited Dr. Martin Luther King Jr. for their Great March to Freedom in 1963. Thousands of peaceful **demonstrators** in Detroit heard an early version of Dr. King's famous "I Have a Dream" speech before he gave it in Washington, D.C. A few years later, demonstrations in Detroit would not be so peaceful. Dr. King urged his followers to work peacefully toward equality, but African Americans became frustrated with **discrimination** in Detroit and throughout the country.

Even metal bars could not stop angry rioters in Detroit. The rioters later burned the buildings they had damaged.

Motown

One of the positive outcomes of the 1960s in Detroit was the Motown Sound. It became a music style that would bring fame and fortune to recording artists like Diana Ross and the Supremes, Smokey Robinson and the Miracles, Marvin Gaye, and Stevie Wonder. They recorded their music in Studio A at Hitsville U.S.A., a building that serves as a **historical** museum about this musical **era.** During the 1960s, the music recorded here became a popular music style heard all over the nation.

A LEADER FROM MICHIGAN

The African American struggle for equality continued in Michigan and throughout the nation in the 1970s. Along with civil rights issues, the 1970s were known as a decade of problems, especially in Washington, D. C. In 1973, congressman and speaker of the House of Representatives, Gerald R. Ford Jr. stepped up to the vice presidency when President Nixon's first vice president, Spiro Agnew, **resigned.** Then, as vice president, Ford became the 38th president of the United States after President Richard Nixon resigned in 1974. Ford was the only vice president and president who was not elected to either position. Before he became the vice president, he had represented Michigan in the United States **Congress** for 25 years.

Gerald R. Ford Jr.

150 YEARS OF STATEHOOD

On January 26, 1987, Michigan celebrated 150 years of statehood. The day's celebrations began in Sault Ste.

Marie, Michigan's oldest continuous settlement, with a 26-gun salute and a dogsled ride. In Lansing, the official Michigan Statehood Stamp was issued. At noon, ceremonies were held in the State **Capitol** building and in every county in the state.

LIFE SCIENCES CORRIDOR

In 1999, Governor John Engler signed a bill for $1 billion to fund a "**life sciences** corridor" in Michigan. This money is used by three Michigan universities and the Van Andel Institute in Grand Rapids to do research on medicine and technology. Over 50 new companies have started in Michigan since the beginning of the project, employing over 20,000 people. The goal of this project is to improve health care by taking advantage of recent developments in technology.

MICHIGAN: A PLEASANT PENINSULA

Michigan has been explored for 13,000 years. The first **nomads** found land rich in natural resources, and today approximately 9,938,000 people call Michigan home. Bordered by four of the Great Lakes, Michigan still holds historical memories of previous generations. Michigan residents have seen the state through tough and good times, and the ideas of future generations will continue to change the place they call home.

Many people enjoy the beautiful sunsets over Lake Michigan.

Map of Michigan

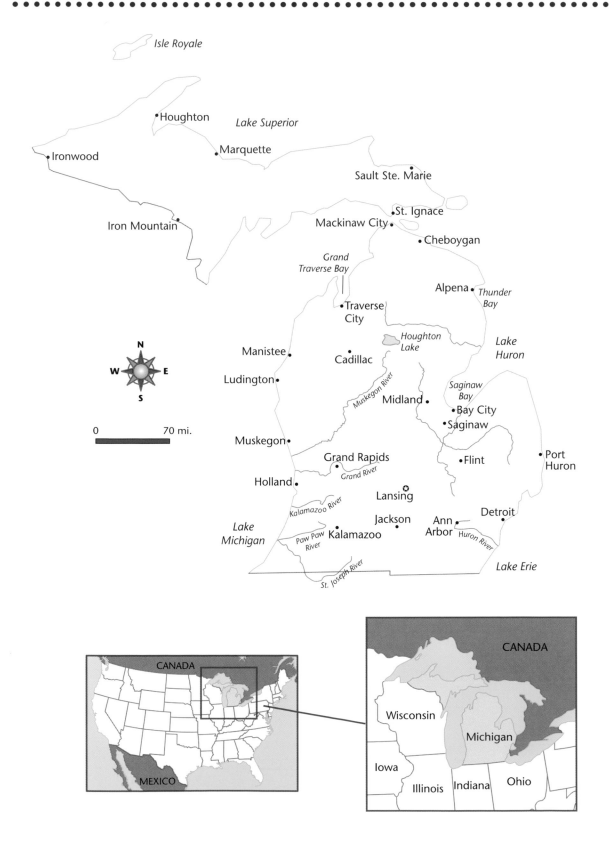

Timeline

20,000 B.C.E.	Earliest people arrive on the continent of North America.
8,000–500 B.C.E.	Last **Ice Age** ends and the **Archaic** People arrive. Old Copper Indians mine copper.
800 B.C.E.	Woodland Peoples: The early moundbuilders known as the Hopewell Indians settle.
About 1622 C.E.	Champlain, a French explorer, travels the Great Lakes. He sends Étienne Brulé to Lake Superior. Many French explorers and priests come to the Michigan region in search of a waterway to China.
1668	Father Jacques Marquette establishes a **mission** at Sault Ste. Marie.
1701	**Fort** Pontchartrain du De Troit (Detroit) founded.
1763	Pontiac's **Rebellion** occurs.
1787	Northwest **Ordinance** passed.
1805	Michigan Territory created with its first **capital** in Detroit.
1812	Fort Mackinac and Fort Detroit are surrendered by the British.
1825	The Erie Canal opens and helps link Michigan with the eastern states.
1835	Ohio and Michigan disagree over the Toledo Strip. This conflict delays Michigan's entry into statehood.
1837	Michigan becomes 26th state with a capital in Detroit and Stevens Mason as first governor.
1847	The state capital moves to Lansing.
1855	The first Soo **Locks** open.
1900	Grand Rapids is the Furniture Capital of the World. Kellogg's and Post cereals from Battle Creek became common breakfast food.
1908	Henry Ford's Model T is manufactured in Detroit.
1935	Auto Workers of America (UAW) is formed.
1957	The Mackinac Bridge opens.
1963	Martin Luther King Jr. speaks in Detroit, urging for peaceful demonstrations during the Civil Rights movement.
1974	Gerald Ford becomes the 38th president of the United States and the only U.S. president from Michigan.
1987	Michigan celebrates 150 years of statehood.
1999	**Life Sciences** Corridor bill is signed.

Glossary

abolition ban slavery. A person who wanted to ban slavery was called an abolitionist.

alliance agreement between two groups to support and protect each other

Allies nations that support each other during times of war. During World War I, Britain, France, and Russia were the Allies.

ammunition objects, such as bullets, fired from guns

archaeologist person who studies history through the things that people have made or built

architect person who designs buildings and gives advice on their construction

artifact something created by humans for a practical purpose during a certain time period

assassinated murder of an important person by surprise attack

assembly plant place where parts are put together to make complete products

barge broad boat with a flat bottom used mainly in harbors and on rivers and canals

board feet lumber measurement. One board foot measures one foot long, one foot wide and one inch thick

bounty hunter someone who is given money as a reward for capturing people or animals

capital location of a government

capitol building in which the lawmakers meet

caribou large deer

Catholicism original church of Christianity centered in Rome, Italy

census count and the gathering of information about a population

climate weather conditions that are usual for a certain area

Congress chief lawmaking body of the United States

conserve planned management of natural resources to prevent waste, destruction, or neglect

constitution basic beliefs and laws of a nation or state in which the powers and duties of government are established and certain rights are guaranteed to the people

cultural ideas, skills, arts, and a way of life of a certain people at a certain time

delegate person sent to a meeting to represent a community

demonstrators group of people who gather to show that they hold a certain opinion

depression time when businesses are doing poorly

deserter someone who leaves without permission or telling anyone

discrimination unfair treatment of people based on their differences from others

diversity having variety

era important period in history

fertile bearing crops or vegetation in abundance

fort strong building used for defense against enemy attack

glacier large sheet of ice that spreads or retreats very slowly over land

historic recorded in history

honorable discharge leave the military service with a good service record

Ice Age period of colder climate when much of North America was covered by thick glaciers

immigrant one who moves to another country to settle

inaugural address speech made by a person before taking office

industry group of businesses that offer a similar product or service

legislator member of a governmental body that makes and changes laws

life science science dealing with living matter such as biology and medicine

lock enclosure with gates on each end used to raise or lower boats as they pass from level to level

mastodon prehistoric relative of today's elephant

migrate move from one place to another

mineral solid substance formed in the earth by nature and obtained by mining

missionary person who travels to spread religious teachings. The building they live in is called a mission.

nomad hunter who moved from place to place, following the herds of wild animals

ordinance law or regulation especially of a city or town

ore rock or mineral from which a metal can be obtained

petroglyph ancient carving on rock

prehistoric from the time before history was written

rebellion opposition to authority

resigned give up by an official act

riot outbreak of wild violence on the part of a crowd

rural having to do with the country or farmland

segregate set one type of people apart from others

treason crime of going against the government

union organization of workers to help them get better working conditions

women's rights movement movement to gain equal rights for women

More Books to Read

Barenblat, Rachel, and Jean Craven. *Michigan the Wolverine State*. Cleveland: World Almanac Education, 2002.

Brill, Marlene Targ. *Michigan*. Tarrytown, N.Y.: Benchmark Books, 1998.

Heinrichs, Anne. *Michigan*. Minneapolis: Compass Point Books, 2003.

Van Frankenhuysen, Gijsbert, and Kathy-Jo Wargin. *The Legend of Mackinac Island*. Chelsea, Mich.: Sleeping Bear Press, 1999.

Index

About the Author

Award-winning photographer and journalist Marcia Schonberg is the author of travel guides, nonfiction children's books, and the Heinemann Library Ohio State Studies books. She has contributed to *Michigan Living* and writes regularly for daily newspapers and regional and national magazines. A mother of three, Marcia resides in the Midwest with her husband Bill and golden retriever, Cassie.